Inspirir

Wome

Every Day

021

May

THE YES'S OF GOD

RACHEL WRIGHT

June

THE SACRED
EVERYDAY

ELISABETH PIKE

MIX
Paper from
responsible sources
FSC® C021017
www.fsc.org

WAVERLEY ABBEY
RESOURCES

Trading name of **CWR**

Rachel Wright

Rachel Wright is a nurse, author of two books, speaker and mum of three boys, one with life-limiting disabilities. She is founder of Born at the Right Time and passionate about bridging the gap between faith and reality. She runs so she can eat more crisps and cake.

Elisabeth Pike

Elisabeth Pike is a writer and designer. *Voice at the Window*, a collection of 100 gratitude poems written during lockdown is out now. *Circles: Nurture and Grow your Creative Gift* was released in April 2019. Her prints and books are available via her Etsy shop, **etsy.com/uk/shop/LittleBirdEditions**

Copyright © Waverley Abbey Resources 2021. Published by Waverley Abbey Resources. Waverley Abbey Resources is a trading name of CWR, Waverley Abbey House, Waverley Lane, Farnham, Surrey GU9 8EP, UK. Tel: 01252 784700

Registered Charity No. 294387. Registered Limited Company No. 1990308.

Front cover image: istockphoto.com

The opinions expressed in this publication are those of the authors and do not necessarily represent the views of the Publisher.

Concept development, editing, design and production by Waverley Abbey Resources. Printed in England by Yeomans. All rights reserved. No part of this publication may be reproduced, stored in a retrieval system, or transmitted, in any form or by any means, electronic, mechanical, photocopying, recording or otherwise, without the prior permission in writing of Waverley Abbey Resources. Unless otherwise indicated, all Scripture references are from the Holy Bible, New International Version® Anglicised, NIV® Copyright © 1979, 1984, 2011 by Biblica, Inc.® Used by permission. All rights reserved worldwide. Scripture quotations marked The Message are taken from THE MESSAGE, copyright © 1993, 2002, 2018 by Eugene H. Peterson. Used by permission of NavPress. All rights reserved. Represented by Tyndale House Publishers, Inc.

The Yes's of God

RACHEL WRIGHT

....

Jeremiah 17:5–8

'They will be like a tree planted by the water that sends out its roots by the stream.' (v8)

The past year has upended us. Our priorities, perspective and perception of normal have been changed – probably forever. We are learning to live in a new way, having had our default settings halted and reset. This kind of dramatic, uninvited relearning is rarely welcome or comfortable. But with everything in life, although we don't always get to choose what happens, we do get the opportunity to choose how we respond.

In a stressful situation there are the commonly known 'fight or flight', reactions which emerged from research in the 1920s. However, this research was found to have a gender bias, and once women were included in studies, a paper published in 2000 showed females have a 'tend and befriend' response.* Women rise up when put under pressure. They engage in activities, which reduce stress and promote safety for self and offspring, and they build networks which help facilitate this response. When your faith, health, circumstances or relationships are under pressure, what practices relieve stress and develop healthy networks?

....

Optional further reading
Annie Lammott, *Help, Thanks, Wow: The Three Essential Prayers*

**2 Corinthians
1:12–22**

'For no matter how many promises God has made, they are "Yes" in Christ. (v20)

Are you **sure**?

Growing up, during the troubles in Northern Ireland, I thought being a Christian meant a whole load of no's. No swearing, no listening to pop music, no make-up, no dating (pretty sure my dad made that one up) – basically no fun at all. Looking back, although my parents' heart for Jesus was much bigger, my teenage self heard the restrictions louder than the invitations. My faith had a tendency to tie me up rather than set me free.

Forty years later, I wonder whether I'm still inclined to zone in on the no's. As a parent, I can certainly find myself saying no more than yes on any given day. I wonder if this uninvited default continues to taint my view of faith and God. Am I anticipating a bearded white man in the sky raising his hand and saying, 'STOP!' whenever I get close to enjoying myself?

In the not-too-distant past, I believed being the person God wanted me to be required me being 'less-than': less noisy, less opinionated, less confrontational – just less. But I have been challenged to flip my narrative of God and instead of getting stuck in the treacle of no's, I stepped into the freedom of yes's. Maybe God is all about more rather than less – more love, hope, rest, fun, laughing and joy – with a whole lot more grace, patience, tears, silence and tenderness. Quite simply, maybe God wants us to stop fighting, fleeing, shrinking or tying ourselves up with no's. He's just waiting for us to find the freedom of yes and start growing into all He created us to be.

Over the next month, we'll be looking at God's yes's and the ways women of faith, often amidst turmoil, said yes to God.

**For prayer
and reflection**

**Lord, help me to
think about how I
view my faith – full
of no's or yes's. As
I step into today
and the coming
days, help me to
see where You are
saying yes in my
life. Amen.**

Reading God's Word with **curiosity**

Psalm 23:1–6

'The LORD is my shepherd... he leads me beside quiet waters, he refreshes my soul.' (vv1–3)

I once viewed the Bible as my manual to life: a kind of framework that told me the rights and wrongs I needed to keep in step with God. In Sunday school, I learnt memory verses, which remain planted in my brain thanks to the bribery of sweets, stickers and even hard cash. Having followed Jesus all my life, the Bible contains well-known verses. Where once I might skip over them, believing I already had them in the bag, these days I'm trying to hold the word of God with greater reverence and much less black and white thinking.

The world of Jesus' time, holds cultural and spiritual practices that are alien to me. When 400-year-old Shakespeare baffles me, it is no surprise that the subtleties and complexities of words written 2,000 years ago can't simply be lifted into twenty-first century Britain without considered application, thought and reflection.

When we open God's Word, we are opening up the power of stories. The lives of both men and women are recorded as making up part of God's story and our collective history. These accounts are the heartbeat of God on earth.

The Bible isn't a science textbook, nor a psychology self-help guide, it is the opportunity to eavesdrop on the story of God and His people written by men in a certain time and specific place. Throughout the centuries, it has been interpreted, edited and shaped. And here's the miracle: now, today, with the help of the Holy Spirit, a curious mind and open heart, we can wrestle with, question and lean on God's Word. We can allow it to open our eyes, knowing it has survived thus far and will not break.

For prayer and reflection

God, help me to be curious and see things from a different perspective; to have the confidence to ask questions, start conversations, believing it will restore my soul. Amen.

....

Matthew 5:1–11

....

'Now when Jesus saw the crowds, he went up on a mountainside and sat down.' (v1)

Sermon on the Mount: yes or no

When Jesus' is chronicled to have spoken His most clearly recorded and detailed sermon, He does so on a mountain with His friends. It is a powerful reminder that God is often in the business of flipping our viewpoint and expectations, easing us into uncharted territory.

Jesus starts with a list of things that I would mostly likely decline with a polite 'No, thank you.' I would like to avoid struggles but the Beatitudes tell me that within them I can find blessings of God – not through their omission but in their presence. The way in which Jesus simply shares these words expresses His passion for yes over no.

When Jesus had something important to say He often went to the mountainside. The Temple might have seemed the best place to assert Jesus' growing popularity as a rabbi, but with the Temple came restrictions. By stepping up the mountain, Jesus was saying yes to everyone, including the women. The yes of Jesus' words was amplified by His actions. Jesus stepped away from the religious establishment and up the mountain to show His heart for the inclusion of women, the marginalised and non-religious.

Then Jesus sat down to talk. He wasn't standing, shouting at the crowd. Jesus 'sat down' with His disciples. This would have been the larger group of men and women who knew Jesus and loved Him. The ones who were ready to give up their lives to walk alongside Him every day. Whereas the crowd may have wanted miracles, Jesus' disciples were ready to listen and learn. The words Jesus spoke were uttered in the context of friendship and founded on relationships of love and trust.

....

For prayer and reflection

....

Thank You, God, for inviting me up the mountain without the rules and limitations of religion. Help me to listen and learn on whatever mountainside I meet You today. Amen.

WAVERLEY ABBEY TRUST

COLLEGE · RESOURCES · HOUSE

verleyabbeycollege.ac.uk   waverleyabbeyresources.org   waverleyabbeyhouse.org

Waverley Abbey Trust

We are a charity serving Christians around the world with practical resources and teaching. We support you to grow in your Christian faith, understand the times in which we live, and serve God in every sphere of life.

The five main areas we focus on are:

- **Bible Engagement**
- **Prayer**
- **Mental Wellbeing**
- **Leadership**
- **Spiritual Formation**

waverleyabbey.org

It isn't that **simple**

Matthew 6:25–30

'Therefore… do not worry about your life, what you will eat or drink; or about your body, what you will wear.' (v25)

Any sentence that starts with 'Therefore' needs to be read in context with the sentence before. The passage before asks us where our allegiance lies: with God or money, because it can't be both. This is the spring board from which Jesus instructs the crowd to not worry about what they will eat or wear.

The Sermon on the Mount can read like a lot of no's: 'do not be like the hypocrites' (Matt: 6:5); 'do not look sombre' (v16); 'Do not store up' (v19); 'do not worry' (v25). After all our world has faced over the last year, 'do not worry' is easier said than done. Yet, look closer and things are more complex. In verse 17, Jesus instructs those gathered to put oil on their hair and wash their face when they fast. In other words, He's telling them to look good so others don't know they are fasting. Then only 12 verses later, Jesus is saying not to worry about clothes and food. Scripture isn't always crystal clear but rather reflects the complexity of life then and now.

I imagine that, just maybe, a crowd has gathered around Jesus, so He heads up the mountainside to lose all but His closest friends. The sun has been beating down all day, dust is gathering between their toes, and tempers have frayed. Some of the disciples feel they should be eating better. Their growing popularity surely means they should shop in Waitrose rather than Asda. Some of the women are plotting to upgrade Jesus' wardrobe, feeling His current garb isn't befitting a man with growing prestige. The cool breeze of the mountainside is a welcome relief as they sit down to enjoy the view. Then Jesus starts to speak. He speaks as a friend, into their lives. He speaks as someone who loves them and knows their conversations and reality.

For prayer and reflection

What ordinary conversations have you been having this week which Jesus might want to sit on the mountainside and encourage you to step into another way of thinking about?

Step into **peace**

A s a twenty-first century woman, I'm not overly surprised Jesus didn't worry about food or clothes. My husband has only recently taken over the duty of our family's shopping, but still he is not that interested in what he wears. In first-century Jewish homes, men were not typically worried about these things either. Yet today, indicated by the number of foodbanks working in our communities, we all know that people go hungry. And despite Jesus using the birds of the air as an illustration for provision, BBC nature documentaries show the brutality of climate change and the suffering wildlife as a result.

I suspect that what Jesus is talking about here is bigger than cultural norms, poverty, environmental issues or shopping lists. By looking beyond, 'Do not,' Jesus is inviting us into a deeper calling related to how we really nourish our bodies and what sets us apart from others.

It seems Jesus' followers – then and now – fell into the trap of thinking what they ate and what they wore defined them. Could Jesus still be calling His followers into that deeper freedom founded on a bigger yes by challenging us with what we spending our time dwelling on?

Think: what is your first thought of the day? 'What is for breakfast?' 'What's on the news?' Or 'what can bring me deeper into the peace and purpose of God?' The flowers of the field that Jesus describes in verse 28 are small and vibrant wildflowers, which grow amidst the golden fields of wheat. Instead of clothing, Jesus is asking us to consider what aspects of our lives set us apart. What is springing up in our lives, which vibrantly shows His beauty to others?

Matthew 6:30–34

'If that is how God clothes the grass of the field… will he not much more clothe you…?'
(v30)

For prayer and reflection

What are the things in your life that give a shot of 'Jesus colour' in a field of otherwise autumnal colours?

Inspired all over again

....

Hebrews 4:1–13

'For the word of God is alive and active.' (v12)

I have a confession. For some years, I was scared of the Bible. Despite always having a copy by my bed or on my phone, I started to fear reading God's Word. I worried its pages might shake my faith so hard it would slip through my fingers completely. The stories of misogyny, sexual abuse, slavery and violence turned my stomach and made me weep.

Then I read Rachel Held Evans's book, *Inspired*. Rachel shares her reverence for God's ordained Word, spoken to His people at a specific time in a particular place. It has been like a breath of fresh air in my stumbling walk with Jesus. I am tentatively, respectfully, humbly re-reading words, which have reverberated in my ears for decades. I have heard God's voice anew in the unfolding story of His people lurching and leaning into a future.

I am hopeful and expectant that God's story is not yet finished. It is not locked in the pages of a 2,000-year-old text. It is living and anointed with the unending power of the Holy Spirit, constantly challenging God's people to break boundaries, and gently leading us into new and unexpected places.

....

Optional further reading
Rachel Held Evans, *Inspired*

Questionable women

'This is the genealogy of Jesus the Messiah the son of David, the son of Abraham' (v1)

The cultural differences reflected in Scripture compared to today are breath taking. Even the genealogy of Jesus presents questions by listing a host of remarkable, and somewhat questionable, women. Their inclusion is unusual, so it begs the question: why have these women survived the oral-telling, retelling, recording and translating of God's story across the centuries?

There is Bethsheba the Hittite, then Tamar the Canaanite (v3). Tamar tricked Judah into getting her pregnant by pretending to be a prostitute. Then there is Rahab the Canaanite living in Jericho, who appeared to fall under the spell of love at first sight with Salmon saving her from certain death. Their son Boaz married Ruth the Moabite whose son, Obed, is the grandad of King David. Finally there is Mary (v16), a seemingly pure Jewish woman among all these dubious Gentile women. Her virginity and unquestioned heritage are quite the contrast. What might this list of colourful women tell us?

Firstly, we can be thankful that today women (in most places of the world) have more status, opportunity and control over their sexuality and future. Sadly, there are still countries where women's freedom and rights are not respected or protected. There is much work still to do.

Secondly, this list of women is another nod in Scripture to the outsiders and marginalised not only being welcomed in but fundamental to God's plan for the incarnation of Jesus on earth. Love is messy and sex complicated, but it takes all kinds of women to weave together God's remarkable, messy, brilliant story here on earth.

For prayer and reflection

Almighty God, thank You for the women who have come before me; for their stories and their lives. Use me to be a woman in Your kingdom today.

What's the **whole** story?

Luke 2:1–7

'While they were there, the time came for the baby to be born, and she gave birth to her firstborn' (v6)

Sometimes I wonder how different the Bible would read if women had written it. Instead of the census, the journey, the lack of accommodation and unlikely crib, I'd love to know about the conversations, longings, fears and hopes.

Today, when we hear a baby has been born, what information do we initially find out? 'Mother and baby are well', time of birth, weight (which, for some strange reason, we insist on sharing in pounds and ounces).

If we get chance to sit down with a close friend and new mother, we are more likely to find out a lot more intimate details over a cup of tea, laughter and tears. Even in pregnancy and childbirth, there is a cultural incentive to present a clinical, polished version of life. Yet real life is brutal, beautiful and everything in between.

We can be honest here: long before the pressures of putting on a perfect front for Facebook, there was church. Have you ever left home on Sunday morning in an atmosphere so thick you could cut it with a knife? Then once inside church everything changes. Maybe it's the Holy Spirit – or maybe a longing to portray a better side of ourselves.

There is so much missing in Mary's story. So many details I would love to know – ideally sitting and laughing with her over a cup of tea. But one thing we know that Mary clearly did, as described in Scripture, is say a loud and resounding yes. She said yes to the angel (eventually), yes to Joseph (enthusiastically, maybe hesitantly), yes to her cousin Elizabeth (with a big sigh of relief). Her heart was constantly open and ready to be stretched into more and more of God's yes'. Whether it was messy, unpredictable, uncomfortable – or beautiful.

For prayer and reflection

What story are you telling at the minute that is the shiny version? Tell someone you trust the whole truth today.

An **ordinary** and **extraordinary** yes

"'I am the Lord's servant," Mary answered. "May your word to me be fulfilled.'" (v38)

Growing up as a Protestant in Northern Ireland, Mary firmly belonged to my Catholic neighbours in a way I didn't really understand. In whichever version, the Bible honours Mary. I once heard Nadia Bolz-Weber question whether this reverence of Mary was an attempt by the men of the day to paint her as 'other'. She couldn't just be an ordinary woman because women were less-than, unworthy, unpredictable, over emotional beings. At the time of Jesus' birth, women struggled to live well without the authority of a man. They couldn't own land and their lineage wasn't counted. But Mary was different to other women. Maybe that is why she is so prominent in this tale. Her difference set her apart and made her extraordinary.

Except maybe not.

Despite the huge cultural differences (that I cannot begin to comprehend) some bits would still be the same. Mary would have been woken at night by her baby's crying to be fed. Like every other woman on this planet who has nursed a child, it would be a time to think and dream as darkness cloaked the night.

I'm sure Mary said no sometimes. She was an ordinary, as well as extraordinary, woman after all. But her yes to the angel Gabriel made a difference in a history-changing, heaven-opening, world-transforming way. I don't think she could have predicted that.

I'm confident we can't always anticipate the impact of our yes's or no's. But when we open ourselves up to a yes in God, with all our femininity, womanhood and wonderful ordinariness, what He is able to do is mind blowing – just ask Mary.

For prayer and reflection

Heavenly Father, take my stumbling, ordinary and extraordinary yes as a woman of God and break into this world in new, more powerful ways. Amen.

Yes, to the **moment**

Luke 2:22–32

'Moved by the Spirit, he went into the temple courts.' (v27)

Cloaked with uncertainty, fatigue and the bewilderment of new motherhood, the teenage mother, Mary, walked the two-hour trek to the Temple at Jerusalem from Bethlehem with her husband and baby to keep the law when Jesus was 40 days old.

Joseph may have already taken Jesus to a local synagogue in Bethlehem for His *brit milah* (v21). This occurs eight days after a child's birth, and is the covenantal circumcision and naming ceremony. It is a ritual which firmly places the child within the Jewish community. Rabbi Debra Orenstein says, 'The infant is transformed, named, given tribe and history, roots and purpose, baggage and wings."

However, today was Mary's day of purification rites required by Jewish law, and being so close to the awesome Temple in Jerusalem it was obviously an opportunity too good to miss. By any architectural or religious standards, the Temple in Jerusalem has a grandeur and holiness, which remains the centre of passionate allegiance to this day. Maybe Joseph had been there many times, having grown up only five miles away, but who knows how many times the young woman from Nazareth had made the 150-kilometre walk.

At 40 days, the whole family are able to enter the Temple when Mary is purified and deemed clean. And that is how long the Holy Spirit waits before prompting Simeon to go to the Temple too. Simeon allowed his feet to walk in the yes, giving Mary a message — one she needed to hear. It was a time when all the pieces seemed to fit together to create that much needed interaction.

For prayer and reflection

Guide me, Lord, lead me and let my words, my steps be anointed by You. Amen.

'Rabbi Jane Rachel Litman and Rabbi Debra Orenstein, *Lifecycles Volume 2: Jewish Women on Biblical Themes in Contemporary Life* (Jewish Lights Publishing, 1998) pp61–62

Yes, to being more like **Anna**

Luke 2:33–40

'Coming up to them at that very moment, she gave thanks to God and spoke about the child' (v38)

Simeon had a lot to say, and the men who wrote Scripture recorded his crafted words. Centuries later, they are still spoken in churches today. But Anna is my personal favourite in this scene.

The translation and re-interpretation of Scripture sometimes loses some of the vibrancy and colour of the characters. In recording one kind of detail, I think we have glossed over some of the heart and soul of the wonderful lives being unfolded. Yet Anna still stands out. She was clearly devout and respected. She may well have stayed in the Temple in order to survive as a widow without financial support. The actual words of Anna are not recorded, despite her being a prophet. This might have been because Anna's words weren't considered important enough but I'd like to think it's because she spoke too fast, too excitedly or too long. I love to imagine – in the hustle and bustle and enormity of Jerusalem's Temple – Anna's spark, animation, life and eccentricity livened up the purification proceedings dramatically.

But what I love most about Anna is that despite the stark, bare bones of Jesus' birth, she is still included and remains a character 2,000 years later. Her spiritual fervor, her connectedness and devotion superseded her social standing as a widow and a descendent of Zilpah (the handmaiden of Leah). All because she said yes to God every day – praying, fasting and living in the Temple.

In return, God breathed yes into her every day. So much so, Anna would talk about Jesus 'to all who were looking forward to the redemption of Jerusalem' (v38).

For prayer and reflection

Almighty God, give me the heart, eyes, ears and words of Anna – devoted to speaking Your truth to anyone who will listen. Amen.

Yes, to rest

....

Exodus 20:8–11
'Remember the Sabbath day by keeping it holy.' (v8)

'How are you?'

'Oh, I'm just so busy!'

How often have you partook in the 'Busy Olympics'? In a culture where worth equals productivity, being busy has been a gold standard (although 2020 made many of us stop).

God calls us to work but I believe He also calls us to pleasure, fun and rest. When it comes to the Old Testament commandments (designed to lead Israel deeper into God), keeping one day a week holy made it into the Top 10. If I had ten things to tell my 13-year-old son, 'don't work' wouldn't be one of them. But we cannot ignore the wonderful truth that God commands us to rest. In order to create a day that is holy, He tells us we must stop the hustle, and honour Him in resting.

For me, my Sabbath hasn't landed on a Sunday for years. Whether preparing for a worship group or getting three children (one who is severely disabled) ready for church, Sunday is most definitely work. So, my Sabbath is carved out at different times of the week. In these verses, I hear the heartbeat of God saying yes to margins and space where, in the stillness, the quiet of His voice can be heard.

....

Optional further reading
Tim and Rachel Wright, *Shattered*

Yes, to **balance**

Luke 6:1–11

'Then Jesus said to them, "The Son of Man is Lord of the Sabbath."' (v5)

'You always take it too far.' I can still hear my dad's words as they echo from my childhood, growing up with two brothers and two sisters. We would be having fun, mucking about, and sure enough, at some point, one of us would start crying because someone did something to someone else. What started out as good healthy fun eventually became destructive and unhelpful.

I have a horrible feeling I have a tendency to pendulum over many things in my life (except exercise – I've never been overly tempted to exercise). What starts off as a fulfilling and good idea, grows until it becomes a little more rigid. Then, before I know it, the thing has begun dictating my life. One thing, which immediately springs to mind, is social media. I start connecting with people, engaging with long-lost friends but then time passes, and before long I have lost hours scrolling and obsessing – checking my feed and other people's stories.

In the passage we read today, Jesus is suggesting this could even be true for our faith practices. Could it even include prayer or going to church? Prayer connects us with God. It connects us to God within us. But there have been times in my life when my lack of structured prayer has fueled guilt and caused fatigue (as I tried to get up earlier and earlier to fit it in). Having rhythm, discipline and spiritual practices as part of every day and week are right and good. But as Jesus cautioned when walking through the field – who is in charge? In the way we conduct our spiritual lives with prayer, attending church or reading Scripture, are we finding freedom or guilt?

For prayer and reflection

Have any of your spiritual practices swung into a regimented burden that stifles rather than liberates? Does anything need to change?

Yes, to **food**

**Matthew
11:1–19**

'Here is a glutton
and a drunkard, a
friend of tax
collectors and
sinners.' (v19)

Have you ever called someone on the phone only to hear, 'Oh, it's you.'? It's not the most welcoming of greetings. and it's one echoed by John's followers: 'Are the one who is to come, or should we expect someone else?' (v3)

John had already baptised Jesus. He'd identified Him as the Messiah but something changes. John was in prison but was this negative tone down to something more than that? Was it because Jesus was just so ordinary, so irreverent and relaxed, a man who liked a drink, friends and food: accused of being 'a glutton and drunkard' (v19)? It does sound in stark contrast to John's discipline and fasting.

I think I have always been led to believe that Jesus was the straitlaced, early riser who didn't step a toe out of line, making Him seem ultimately quiet, somber and preachy. But maybe He is more accurately described as the rebel who loved an evening with a gaggle of friends, eating and drinking.

This is good news to me because I love food. Only the other week, I was telling my husband how my problem isn't that I eat unhealthily because I love healthy food: bean salad, fresh vegetables, a plate full of colour and flavour. The issue is that I love all the carbohydrates too: sugar, starch and fatty foods. His helpful response was, 'So, what you're saying is you just love *all* food.'

'Erm, yes.'

Thankfully, so did Jesus. I bought my dad a mug at Christmas, which said, 'Jesus took naps, be more like Jesus'. Jesus was also known for loving food with His friends. So, I'm being more like Jesus, embracing the beauty and bounty of food, which fills our bodies and stimulates the gatherings of our community.

**For prayer
and reflection**

If possible, make plans this week to eat with someone new. Have a meal, which will nourish your body, mind and spirit.

Yes, to **equity** and **status**

Luke 10:38–42

'he came to a
village where a
woman named
Martha opened
her home to him.'
(v38)

I have read the story of Mary and Martha dozens of times, and recently with an excited heart. I want to explore the lives of these women more in the next few days. Firstly, the fact the story is set in Martha's house is a startling truth. In twenty-first century, Britain this sentence sits idly, unassuming and unimportant. In first-century Bethany (two miles outside Jerusalem), it would have been jaw-dropping and posed many unanswered questions. Women at that time rarely. Held the right to property or land unless she was under the guardianship of a man (father, brother or husband). If a husband died, the land and home would go to the nearest male relative. If she was unmarried (unlikely for a woman beyond her teens), she would remain in her father's house or seek refuge among her other male relatives.

Today when talking about a couple, we would name the man and woman; in the time of Jesus, it was accepted the man would only be named. As no man is named, it is not clear whether Martha is married or not. Yet here is a seemingly wealthy Martha, in her home, inviting and serving guests. Jesus was a dear friend, so it isn't unreasonable to assume He had stayed many times. In the oral telling of this story and the eventual writing of it, the status of these two women remained important enough for men recording the event to acknowledge. It was an incredible statement 2,000 years ago and shines a light on the significant steps Jesus took in challenging assumptions of the time about the role and position of women. I wonder if, 2,000 years later, He is pleased or despondent with our progress in this aspect of His work.

**For prayer
and reflection**

**What men and
women in history
or in your own life
have paved the
way of equality?**

Yes, to our **ministry**

'Mary has chosen what is better, and it will not be taken from her.' (v42)

I f you came to my home today (as I write), you would see my husband do all the cooking, cleaning and caring for our children. But that isn't the whole story because I do the lion share of these things. This simple interaction between Jesus, Mary and Martha in today's reading has a distinct narrative. There is the beavering, domestic servant and the attentive, contemplative disciple. With the inadequacy of detail comes the reality that there will be so much more we don't know about these women.

When Jesus congratulates Mary for listening at His feet, it flies in the face of what was expected of women at the time. The revolutionary context is not only that one woman ran her own home, but the other woman abandoned her assumed role to sit with the men, to listen and learn from the rabbi.

Imagine if Mary was frustrated by Martha's busyness. Would Jesus' response have been different if Mary had challenged Martha's behaviour? Maybe the problem wasn't how either Mary or Martha behaved but rather that one woman challenged the other to be more like her.

Too often my own fears of inadequacy are fueled by women living with different priorities to mine. Yet I realise diversity should be encouraged by us building each other up rather than tearing down. We are called to cheer each other on because there is no scarcity in God's kingdom. There is room and opportunity for us all to live our lives of ministry and connection in a way that suits our personalities and values. We find freedom in being each other's cheerleaders, celebrating the diversity of God's work as we are dedicated to encouraging the variety of our complex, fully authentic selves.

For prayer and reflection

Over the coming days, deliberately contact some of your female friends with the sole purpose of encouraging what they are doing.

Yes, to **humour**

John 11:1–16

I love Thomas. He's unfairly dubbed the doubter despite none of the other men initially believing the women's reports of Jesus' resurrection either.

I also love humour, satire and laughing so hard my stomach hurts while tears streak down my face. I am absolutely confident that, as in every group of men and women, those following Jesus would have included every personality type – even the joker.

My husband is a quiet, thoughtful, hardworking doctor. Get him together with our university friends, however, and the in-jokes, caricature behaviour and jovial jaunts down memory lane abound. For the disciples, I can only imagine that living on the road together for years would brew hilarity equal to six years in medical school.

The relationships between Jesus and His followers were forged in a passionate, revolutionary time. They created memories, witticisms and group dynamics. I'm sure their conversations would have been poignant and earnest but also lighthearted mundane and full of banter. Today's key verse makes me wonder if Thomas oiled their time together with teasing and dramatic sarcasm.

Lazarus had died, and Jesus declares He's going back to Bethany to 'wake him up' (v11). (Jesus has to spell out he means raise him from the dead). There is concern amongst the group because Jesus was nearly stoned when they were last near Jerusalem, but He insists that they need to go back. The air is thick with grief and fear. As I see it, Thomas, ever hopeful to lighten the mood, interjects, 'Let us also go, that we may die with him.' Maybe he meant it sincerely or maybe he said it with a side-ways smirk, hoping to break the tension and make everyone smile.

> 'Then Thomas… said to the rest of the disciples, "Let us also go, that we may die with him."' (v16)

For prayer and reflection

Lord, thank You that our lives contain fun. Help us to cherish humour, seek out laughter and cultivate smiles – especially when grief and fear lingers close by. Amen.

Yes, to hesitancy and grief

....

John 11:17–32

'When Martha heard that Jesus was coming, she went out to meet him, but Mary stayed at home.' (v20)

My brother is dead. The weeping mourners cannot penetrate the hole in my heart. One man could have prevented the tumour of grief consuming me but Jesus did not come. Now Lazarus is dead. Martha has gone to greet Him but it is too late. He is too late

Mary is emotive, passionate, absorbed and sullen. Martha is practical, determined and busy. Martha runs to greet Jesus because there is nothing else that she can do. Mary remains at home consumed in grief.

The conversation between Jesus and Martha shows that she believes a miracle is still possible (v22) and Lazarus will be raised again in the last day (v24). Jesus and Martha stand, eyes locked, as Martha proclaims she is looking at the Messiah (vv25–26).

Mary's interaction is quite different. She falls to the ground and simply says, 'Lord, if you had been here, my brother would not have died' (v32). There is no hope, no possible miracle, no proclamation of sovereignty.

Two women spoke with Jesus in their truest, authentic selves, full of doubt, hope, grief and dismay. Jesus met each one with compassion and love, exactly where they were.

....

Optional further reading

Barbara Brown Taylor, *Learning to walk in the dark*

New book for women from Jen Baker

An extract from the introduction of Jen Baker's latest book

One of the most profound truths in the Bible is that regardless of how we came into this world – whether by love, passion or violence – we were chosen. God is intentional and at the moment of creation you were not only His first choice, but His best choice. At birth, He knew the number of hairs on your head (or lack thereof) and the number of days before you. God is responsible for bringing us into the world, but what we do with that time – and the legacy we choose to leave – is solely our responsibility.

Choice was created at the birth of Creation. The first Hebrew word of the Bible means 'in the beginning' and the second means God (Elohim), with the third word, bara, meaning 'created'. Any type of creation, whether we are creating a meal or a memory, involves choice. Therefore, Elohim chose, before time was established, to express His love by appointing mankind as the recipient of His love; because love without an object to love is unfulfilled, empty and void of purpose. In other words, you are God's desire!...

My prayer is that as you read, fear will lose its grip, faith will come alive, and purpose will be realigned… positioning you for a lifetime of relentless, kingdom pursuit.

This is your time, and this is your choice – make it an unwavering one.

Want to keep reading?
Visit **waverleyabbeyresources.org.uk/product/unwavering** to order.

Yes, to our **senses**

John 12:1–8

'Then Mary took about half a litre of pure nard, an expensive perfume; she poured it on Jesus' feet' (v3)

A fter Lazarus was raised from the dead, many people believed (John 11:45) but the chief priests and Pharisees start to plot Jesus' death (vv47–53). Then, one week before Jesus dies, He is eating with His friends as the celebrated guest of honour. Lazarus is reclining, maybe telling people what it is like to die. Martha is happily feeding people, and Mary is her exuberant, sensitive self. There is no tension as each member of the family willingly lives their own purpose.

I have a very poor sense of smell, lurching from hay-fever in summer to allergic rhinitis in winter. However, if I had walked into Martha's house that day, I think I would have smelt freshly cooked bread and meat over the fire. The aroma of olives and figs might have punctured the air and stimulated my taste buds with a sweetness and salt. The men and women whose dusty sandals remained at the door and cleanly washed feet reclined at the table. Some could have done with more than just their feet being washed as sweaty clothes hung off warm bodies. All while children played in the courtyard.

Amidst the cacophony of sights, sounds and smells in walks Mary and, in a custom described frequently in literature at the time, she honors Jesus by anointing His feet. Except this time, when the nard drips through His toes and onto the floor, she wipes it with her hair. It's an excessive, expensive expression of devotion. A common act used to honour a man, amplified by extravagance and intimacy. Did Mary know what Jesus was on the verge of? Whatever the motivation, Mary's anointing of Jesus is a beautiful, frivolous, personal, explosion to the senses.

For prayer and reflection

Lord, thank You for the beauty and eruption of our senses alongside the opportunities for extravagance and celebration. Amen.

Yes, to **creativity**

D orcas (or, as Peter calls her, Tabitha) was always doing good and helping the poor. As her friends and family were grieving her death, they heard Peter was in the neighbourhood and called for him immediately. Peter enters the wailing house with the widows jostling to demonstrate the magnitude of their loss by exhibiting the beautiful garments made by Tabitha when she was alive. The fashion she crafted, garments that she had exquisitely woven and sewed to bring elegance and splendor to their community. Tabitha was a creator and what she made was exceptional.

Too often I get bogged down by my to-do list, too busy to give credit or value to creativity and beauty. Yet creating beauty can be one of our most holy activities. We have been created to create by the greatest of all creators. God's design and passion for magnificence and opulence in the magnitude and finite detail of nature is undeniable.

Art is not given the same importance as mathematics in our education system. Productivity and financial viability are frequently valued over aesthetics in commerce. Spirituality is often celebrated in our church communities more than creativity. But God (and Peter) might have a different perspective. Prayer shawls crocheted by women; bunting sewn by young mothers to mark a celebration; swirling paints etched by tiny fingers; and beautiful clothes worn at a wedding – these are the fabric of what it means to be creatives, called by God to bring life, colour and beauty to His communities here on earth.

....

Acts 9:36–43

....

'All the widows stood… crying and showing him the robes and other clothing that Dorcas had made' (v39)

....

For prayer and reflection

....

Creator God, help me use my hands, my words and my life to bring beauty into Your world. Inspire me and give me courage to take time and share my creator heart. Amen.

Yes, to your **story**

Matthew 28:1–10

'Do not be afraid. Go and tell my brothers to go to Galilee; there they will see me.' (v10)

Tabitha created beautiful clothing crafted with her own hands. The women at the tomb lived through Jesus' ministry and witnessed His resurrection. Mary (the mother of Jesus) had a central role in God's redemptive plan. Esther, although essentially a slave, was the most influential woman in the country (Esther 5v3).

Our ministry or our work is carved from our skills, knowledge, story and circumstances. These women used their yes's to be part of, and lead, a vulnerable community and upside-down kingdom. They were emotional, extravagant, creative, diligent and simple. They spoke their message with their words, work, craft, families and lives.

Our message might change as we walk through the seasons of life. Maybe once we had a house full of children but now, we linger by the phone, waiting for it to ring. It might be our art which brings joy and connection. Maybe it's flavoursome food which we conjure that gathers families and friends. It could be volunteering at a local foodbank, doing the school run, or the millionth pile of laundry. Whether we are directing a company or writing letters to inmates, each of our stories –every aspect of our lives – is an important piece of God's story.

Sometimes the message is covert (Tamar, Rahab) or obvious (Mary). It might be productive (Tabitha) or powerful (Esther). But each woman is called to connect the reality of their stories, passions, skills and lives with others and with God. There have been an army of women quietly and triumphantly saying yes to God and His ways on earth. In doing so they have changed the world with unexpected, ordinary and remarkable outcomes. What about you?

For prayer and reflection

Heavenly Father, renew in me Your will for me today in the mundane and the extraordinary. Help me to say yes to You and share my life's message with others. Amen.

Yes, to our **bodies**

Genesis 1:26–31

'So God created mankind in his own image, in the image of God he created them;'
(v27)

Y ou are created in the image of God. His spirit, life, creativity and love are pumping through your veins. God's spirit resides in you and is expressed to the world through your body, which has grown and stretched, flourished and failed.

I am working hard to have a better relationship with my body. I'm trying to drown out the voices of the media and fashion industry which presents airbrushed legs and unwrinkled eyes. I'm also trying not to be solely fueled by cake and tea – it isn't easy. Given the amount of time and energy I have wasted thinking about my body and its flaws, a change in perspective and language is an endeavor worth pursuing.

In her book *Mothers, daughters and body image*, Hillary McBride challenges the unattainable standard of beauty fueled by global misinformation and misogyny. One simple way she suggests we can change the narrative about ourselves is through referring to our bodies as 'she'. I've noticed how toxic my language is when I apply this simple rule. I would not speak about a dear friend or my worst enemy in the same way that I feel about or view my own body at times. My body connects my mind and spirit with the outside world. She hugs my children in the morning and lies with her husband at night. She taps out words on a laptop, hoping they connect with, and encourage, others. She makes food for her loved ones and buys birthday gifts for friends. She fails and weeps, she strives and loves to rest in front of Netflix. She is loyal and hardworking; she is flawed but beautifully unique.

For prayer and reflection

What is your relationship with your body? Try thinking and talking about your body as 'she'.

Hillary McBride, *Mothers, daughters and body image* (Brentwood, TN, USA: Post Hill Press, 2017)

Yes, to our inner **voice**

John 16:29–33

'I have told you
these things, so
that in me you may
have peace.' (v33)

Pope Francis reportedly used the words of Fernando Pessoa when he wrote , 'Remember that to be happy is not to have a sky without a storm, a road without accidents, work without fatigue, relationships without disappointments*.' My prayers used to focus on fixing all that was going on around me; praying away the storms, trials and hurdles. I had the idea that if the tricky circumstances of life improved, well, it would all be better – right?

On reflection, my pursuit of a lack of bumps in the road swam against the tide of Jesus' words, 'In this world, you will have trouble' (v33). Yes, there will be trouble. Yes, Jesus – in the power of His life, death and resurrection – has overcome the world but we still live in the now and not yet. Our peace doesn't come from the world, rather from God's spirit within us and the still quiet (or roaring) voice of our creator.

Beyond the bustle of other people's opinions, advice and assumptions is a knowing, which was planted by your God before you were born. Pope Francis continues, 'Being happy is not a fatality of destiny, but an achievement for those who can travel within themselves.' Listening to that inner voice means not abandoning ourselves but finding the truest, most real sense of peace. It comes about when we shed the expectations of others and even let go of our own perceived expectations of ourselves. The peace Jesus offers has always be found when the created, stops wrestling and contorting. Instead she, the created, stops long enough to hear the voice calling her to be entirely who she really is. Through the stillness of her soul the reflection of God is most vivid.

**For prayer
and reflection**

**Take three minutes.
Try not to conjure
words or
specifically pray.
Simply be still and
know your God.**

*The apocryphal Fernando Pessoa and the imagined Pope Francis, 2015

Weekend

Yes, wherever you are

....

Psalm 90:10–17

'establish the work of our hands for us – yes, establish the work of our hands.' (v17)

Jesus ate at Mary and Martha's table (like Friday night pizza with friends or Sunday roast with family). He spoke about God's love on the mountainside to everyone willing to listen (at the kettle, by the photocopier, at the school gate or in line at Tesco). He spoke to women at the well (kitchen sink) and in the Temple in Jerusalem (at the conference or toddler group).

Jesus' ministry years were packed with miracles and tales deemed so important we are still reading about them 2,000 years later. Yet Jesus lived for over 30 years, and during every minute leading up to His ministry years He was no less the son of God and yet entirely human – whether carving a stool, eating breakfast, praying on the mount, pestering his younger brothers or hanging on the cross.

In every part of your ordinary *and* extraordinary life, Jesus looks you right in the eyes and says your name. Every atom in your body feels seen and loved without shame. Taking you by the hand, He says, 'Now go.' You have things to feel, to be, to love, taste and enjoy. There is so much in the world waiting eagerly for your yes.

....

Optional further reading

Jen Hatmaker, *Fierce, Free and Full of Fire: The Guide to Being Glorious You*

A reluctant **yes**

Exodus 3:1–14

'But Moses said to God, "Who am I that I should go to Pharaoh and bring the Israelites out of Egypt?"' (v11)

I n this series of ways in which God says yes and the women who said yes to Him, I haven't mentioned many of the men in scripture who said yes. Given the majority of the Bible tells the stories of men, there are plenty to choose from. There is also a string of men who said yes but only after digging in their heels and saying no first.

There is Jonah who said no in epic proportions. As it turned out, it required being swallowed up by a large fish before even considering yes to be a viable alternate answer to God's call on his life (Jonah 2:9). Moses took some persuading too. In today's passage, he starts the excuses, and they keep coming. Despite laying prostrate in front of a burning bush with God physically speaking to him, Moses questions God's expectations of him. For Paul, it took a blinding light and several days in darkness (Acts 9:3–9) before he considered that saying yes to God meant yes to Jesus too.

Our yes might be hard won. It might be reluctant and hesitant. Counterintuitively, hopefully our yes will sometimes lead to failure because making mistakes shows we are pushing our boundaries and expanding our abilities. Safety might just be limiting God as He calls us into a yes bigger than we imagined. Maybe it is a new adventure or reaching out to a woman in your block of flats. Maybe it is that career option that you're not quite sure you are ready for. Or a church role you are hesitant to apply for. Maybe it is as radical as saying no to commitments in order to make room for the unexpected yes's God might be calling you into. May the margins you create in your days with no, give way for more yes's in God.

For prayer and reflection

Lord, where are You leading me? What do You want me to say yes to? Show me Your heart and Your ways. Guide me and give me the courage to step further and wider with You. Amen.

Waverley Abbey College

Education that changes lives

Our programmes equip students with the skills and knowledge to release their God-given potential to operate in roles that help people.

Central to all of our teaching is the Waverley Integrative Framework. Built on 50 years of experience, the model emphasises the importance of genuineness, unconditional acceptance and empathy in relationships. The courses we offer range from certificates to Higher Education level.

Counselling

As society begins to realise the extent of its brokenness, we continue to recognise the need to train people to support those who are struggling with everyday life, providing training to equip individuals to become professional counsellors. Whatever their starting point in academic learning, we have a pathway to help all students on their academic journey.

Spiritual Formation

For those wanting to be better equipped to help others on their spiritual journey, this programme provides robust and effective Spiritual Formation training. Students engage with theology, psychology, social sciences, historical studies, counselling, leadership studies and psychotherapy.

For more information about all of our course offerings available, visit **waverleyabbeycollege.ac.uk** or email **admissions@waverleyabbeycollege.ac.uk**

Become part of someone's testimony

Our Bible reading notes are read by hundreds of thousands of people around the world, and *Inspiring Women Every Day* and *Every Day with Jesus* have recently been made free in the UK. We want everyone, whatever their financial means, to have access to these resources that help them walk each day with our Saviour.

Here's what one *Inspiring Women Every Day* reader wrote to us:

I just wanted to send a message to say how much I've appreciated the most recent readings in IWED. They have been insightful, honest and have deeply touched my needs through the work of the Holy Spirit I know.

As we trust in God's provision, we know there are costs to providing this ministry. Do you have a passion for God's Word changing lives? Could supporting this vision be a way in which you serve?

A gift of just £2 a month from you will put daily Bible reading notes into the hands of at least one person who is hungry to know God and experience His presence every day.

Visit **waverleyabbeyresources.org/donate** to become part of someone's testimony, or use the form at the back of these notes.

The Sacred Everyday

ELISABETH PIKE

Matthew
6:25–34

'Look at the birds of the air; they do not sow or reap or store away in barns' (v26)

Jesus' words speak overwhelmingly of the ordinariness of life and this is the stuff of the kingdom of heaven. Luke's version of this famous passage says we are to be 'carefree in the care of God' (Luke 12:22, *The Message*). What a wonderful image! Soaring like the birds, unfettered, unstressed, doing what we do best. But how do we do this? How do we live in touch with heaven in our everyday lives?

Finding the sacred in everyday life isn't for the favoured few, it is how we're all called to live. Brother Lawrence, a seventeenth-century French monk wrote, 'I possess God as peacefully in the bustle of my kitchen... as I do on my knees before the Holy sacrament.'* He brought each problem to God, saying: 'God I should not be able to do that unless you enabled me to do it.'** I love his humility and complete reliance on God. I am currently writing these notes during lockdown while home-schooling three children and looking after a one-year-old baby. Some days feel far from sacred! But this is a message that Jesus repeats to us time and time again. The kingdom of God is here for the taking if only we will reach out and take hold of it. So, this month, let us think about the ways that we can stay in tune with the holy; let us remember that we can pull heaven down into each and every day with our prayers. Let us see, like Brother Lawrence, that even the mundane moments of our lives can be offerings to God because He is with us in everything we do.

*Brother Lawrence, *The Practice of the Presence of God* (London: Hodder and Stoughton, 1981) p84

**Ibid, p23

For prayer and reflection

Thank You, heavenly Father that You call us to live like birds, carefree in the care of God. We bring You today anything that is keeping us tied down. Amen.

The **kingdom** of God

Luke 17:20–24

'God's kingdom is already among you'. (v21, *The Message*)

I love how the Gospels record people asking Jesus over and over again, 'But what *is* the kingdom of God?', and He tells them in riddles and stories, 'It is not what you expect, it's the other way up, be childlike, servant-hearted.' *The Passion Translation* of verse 21 says the kingdom is 'already expanding within some of you.' This kingdom is *Jesus.* He is the mustard seed, the small beginning. His life and teaching show us how to change the world. He invites us to let the seed of His kingdom grow in us. If we accept His invitation then just as the universe is constantly expanding so the kingdom is growing in us – ever growing, never diminishing.

Sometimes it can seem that we are carried along on the tide of life: work, children, church, friends and family. I'm writing this in the wake of the coronavirus pandemic. Before Covid-19, it felt like we were always rushing onto the next thing. And then suddenly, everything was reset, revalued. We reassessed what we wanted our lives to be filled with.

Try picturing your life as an empty glass jar. All the important things are represented as big pebbles. If you put them in the jar first, the smaller things will fill in around them. If you fill the jar up with the little stones first, there won't be room for the big ones. This principle also applies to our priorities and how we use our time.

What are you making room for? What are you sowing into? Where are you wasting time? If we are not intentional about our time, it will get taken away from us. Are you allowing room for the kingdom of God to grow in you?

For prayer and reflection

God, help me to see clearly the things You have given me to do, and those which I can let go of for now. Help me to make room for Your kingdom to grow in me. Amen.

Greatest commandment

**Matthew
22:37–40**

'Love the Lord
your God with
every passion of
your heart… all
the energy of your
being' (v37, TPT)

This is the greatest commandment and the cornerstone on which we can build our lives; not one part of us held back. So how do we do this? Living the sacred every day is realising that God is with us each day, all day long: on the commute, at home with small children, in a difficult meeting. He longs to walk alongside us. Let's turn to Him, invite Him in. When we have a difficult decision to make, when we need wisdom, whether we are brokenhearted or full of joy, let us turn first to God, our friend and Father. Corrie Ten Boom tells the story of meeting her former prison camp guard years after being released from Ravensbrück. The guard asked for her forgiveness but Corrie knew that in her own strength she couldn't forgive. She asked God to help her. As she stretched out her hand towards the guard, she was flooded with God's strength. This is an ultimate example of living the sacred every day. But no matter what challenges we face (big or small), when we allow God to permeate our lives, we no longer live in our strength but in His.

If we find resistance in ourselves, let us ask God for help. Is there any part of your life where you don't really want the kingdom of God? Where you would rather have the kingdom of yourself? Ask God to change your heart so that you can welcome Him in. As Frederick Buechner, an American writer, says, 'Jesus Christ… is king… because again and again he is crowned in the heart of the people who believe in him.'* Each time we turn back to God, and invite Him in, we crown Him again.

**For prayer
and reflection**

**God, show me if I
am holding any
part of my life
back from You.
Help me to
surrender that part
to You, knowing
that You deal
gently with me.
Amen.**

*Frederick Buechner, *Listening to Your Life* (New York: HarperCollins, 1992) p23

Using our time **well**

John 21:1–14

'haven't you any fish?... Throw your net on the right side of the boat and you will find some'(vv5,6)

Jesus gives His disciples some helpful strategy; they listen to Him and it pays off! Can we ask God for His strategy for our lives? When we don't stay in the rest that God intends for us, it can be easy to slip back into a work-mule mindset. We can become frantic with life and work, but this can lead to burnout and isn't an effective use of our time. Heidi Baker has spent her life working with orphans in Africa. She used to work long hours witnessing to people, preaching the gospel and helping with the overwhelming needs that she saw. She became exhausted though, and felt God was asking her to stop. When she resumed visiting after a break, she found that God used her just as much even if she couldn't put as many hours in. She says, 'More is accomplished by spending time in God's presence than by doing anything else.' God's strategy can change our lives! We cannot turn away from the needs in our day, but by focusing first on God, we can use his strategy to direct our time.

We are thinking about stewarding our time today, because, as Annie Dillard says, 'How we spend our days is, of course, how we spend our lives.'' As I have been writing these notes, a slim book by Seneca, a Roman philosopher, leapt of the shelf at me. He says, 'Life is long if you know how to use it.''' God is inviting us to live in the 'unforced rhythms of grace' (Matt. 11:29, *The Message*) instead of the treadmill of life.

For prayer and reflection

Lord, I surrender to You my use of time. Give me wisdom. May I be open to hear Your strategy for my life. Amen.

'Heidi Baker, *Birthing the Miraculous: The Power of Personal Encounters with God to Change Your Life and the World* (Lake Mary, FL, USA: Charisma House, 2014) p20

''Annie Dillard, *The Writing Life* (New York: Harper Perennial, 1990) p32

'''Seneca, *On the Shortness of Life* (London: Penguin, 1997) p2

Gratitude

....

Matthew 14:13–21

'Taking the five loaves and the two fish… he gave thanks and broke the loaves.' (v19)

At the start of 2020, I was struggling with winter blues, so I set myself the challenge of posting one gratitude poem every day on social media during Lent.* Lent turned into lockdown and so I kept going until I reached 100 poems. Finding things to be thankful for each day opened my eyes to see what was there all along. The benefit of being grateful and in the moment is beautifully described in the poem 'The Bright Field' by R.S. Thomas. He says the true gold is neither in looking back or straining ahead but by being in the moment, turning aside, being present. Thankfulness doesn't mean that we don't experience trials or struggles, but it is choosing to be thankful in the midst of them. Life is not perfect. It is not meant to be, and never will be. Life is a journey, and joy can be found in the journey, in the little things – even when everything isn't OK.

In times of difficulty, let's try to give thanks for something every day.

....

Optional further reading:

R.S. Thomas, 'The Bright Field'; any of Mary Oliver's poems.
*You can find the book of poems at
etsy.com/uk/shop/LittleBirdEditions

Luke 12:22–34

'Consider how the wild flowers grow. They do not labour or spin.' (v27)

Seeing: **look!**

Raymond Carver says that 'a writer sometimes needs to be able to stand and gape at this or that thing – a sunset or an old shoe – in absolute and simple amazement.'[1] This looking, again and again is for all of us. It is where gratitude comes from. I find that reading any poem by Mary Oliver makes me love the world a little bit more. It doesn't matter where we live, there is always beauty to be found in the skies, in precious moments with family, in communion with God, in taking time to notice. Watch the birds, listen to the wind rustling the leaves on the trees, smell the earth after it has rained. Let's take in the world around us through a lens of thankfulness. It is a constant reminder of God's faithfulness and love to us – if we remember to look for it. Wild flowers do not labour or spin. When we look around at the natural world, we can see the care and creativity of the creator.

The examen is a spiritual practice of coming closer to God by reflecting on your day. There are five steps: 1. Become aware of God's presence. 2. Review the day with gratitude. 3. Pay attention to your emotions. 4. Choose one feature of the day and pray from it. 5. Look towards tomorrow.[2]

Today, why not take some time to review your day with prayer? And when you next get a chance, remember to look at nature in your corner of the world.

For prayer and reflection

Lord, help me to be reminded of Your faithfulness to me in the world around me. Help me to savour the beauty in this world and not to take it for granted. Amen.

[1] Raymond Carver, 'On Writing', *Fires* (London: Vintage, 2009) p23

[2] Search www.ignatianspirituality.com online for a useful guided version of the examen.

Seeing: what **God** sees

Matthew 6:1–19

'when you pray, go into your room, close the door and pray to your Father, who is unseen.'(v6)

A polished exterior is not the kind of offering that God wants from us. He is asking for the depths of us, the whole of us. In the kingdom of heaven, it is the heart that is important. We look at the outward appearance, but God looks at the heart. When we give or pray or fast, we need to do so discretely. It is easy for external gratitude to become the motivator for our acts, but Jesus says, go to the root of it, don't do things to gain praise from others; do them for God first. Let us be the keeper of holy secrets. Let us bless in secret. Jesus says, 'store up for yourselves treasures in heaven... For where your treasure is, there your heart will be also' (v19). Let's hoard up treasure in heaven; let's count each prayer as an act of worship; let's count each act of generosity as a love gift to God – no matter who knows. Let us fast in secret because if it is an act of worship to God, then it doesn't matter if no one sees.

Out of the overflow of the heart the mouth speaks. Jesus says later in Matthew 7, 'every good tree bears good fruit, but a bad tree bears bad fruit. A good tree cannot bear bad fruit, and a bad tree cannot bear good fruit' (vv17–18). Just as a tree cannot fool the harvester, we cannot fool God. Whatever is in our heart will come out in our behaviour. There are many secret sins – jealousy, unforgiveness or greed – that we might harbour without anyone else even suspecting. No one else but our heavenly Father will see these, and only He knows the freedom we will walk in when we leave them behind!

For prayer and reflection

Lord, help me to remember that You see everything, even the unseen. Thank You that You see my heart. Amen.

Seeing: **shine**

**Matthew
5:14–16**

'You are the light of
the world. A town
built a hill cannot
be hidden' (v14)

What power there is in Jesus' words: you *are* the light of the world! A town on hill *cannot* be hidden! This is our identity as children of the light. And notice, it doesn't say that our light will only shine on our best day or when we haven't sinned for a while. There are no conditions. If we have made the decision to accept Jesus into our hearts, we are transferred 'from the domain of darkness... into the kingdom of the Son he loves' (Col. 1:13). Jesus says, 'let your light shine before others, that they may see your good deeds and glorify your Father in heaven' (Matt. 5:16). It all points to Him. We shine so that God may be glorified. When we become a Christian, it is done, we are transferred. Once we belong to the kingdom of light, we 'walk in the light, as he is in the light' (1 John 1:7). The closer we walk with Jesus, the more we will be like Him. Being known and remembered for shining our light to others is an amazing legacy to leave. If we are children of the light, we cannot help but shine that light – just as the waves cannot stop crashing on the shore and the days and nights cannot stop rolling into each other. A town that shines light means that life is there and that cannot be hidden.

Marianne Williamson says, 'We ask ourselves who am I to be brilliant, gorgeous, talented, fabulous? Actually, who are you not to be? You are a child of God... We are all meant to shine as children do... as we let our own light shine, we unconsciously give others permission to do the same.'

**For prayer
and reflection**

**Heavenly Father,
thank You that
because of Your
light, I am light.
Thank You that I
have been
transferred into
the kingdom of
Your beloved son.
Amen.**

'Marianne Williamson, *A Return to Love: Reflections on the Principles of
'A Course in Miracles'* (New York: HarperOne, 1992) p190

Bouncing Forwards

By Patrick Regan

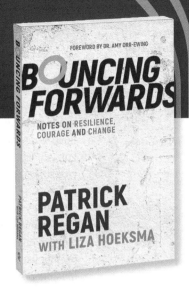

'You'll bounce back.'

Have you ever heard those words? They are always well-meant, but there's one problem: why would we want to bounce back? When what we go through teaches us so much, why would we want to return to how we were before? Perhaps there's a better option. Let's bounce forwards instead.

Explore what true resilience is, and reflect on themes of courage, change and emotional agility as Patrick shares from his own experience and the experiences of others. Readers will also benefit from an included bonus devotional, 'The Resilient Life' by Diane Regan.

'Masterfully woven together' – Tanya Marlow

'A brilliant, timely book for everyone' – Pete Greig

'This book is utterly life-giving' – Will Van Der Hart

'Disarmingly honest and powerfully vulnerable'
– Malcolm Duncan

Start your journey in bouncing forwards today at
waverleyabbeyresources.org/bf

Patrick Regan OBE is Co-Founder of Kintsugi Hope. He is author of six books and speaks regularly on TV and radio on issues of faith, justice and wellbeing.

Seeing: eyes of **faith**

Mark 4:26–29

'This is what the kingdom of God is like. A man scatters seed… the seed sprouts… he does not know how'(vv26,27)

As we walk with Jesus day by day, casting our cares on to Him and following the promptings that He gives us, we are spreading seeds of the kingdom. As if by magic these seeds start to grow. We cannot make them grow, our job is to spread the seeds and God takes care of the rest. I sometimes have to remind myself that God wants to use *me* – as I am, right now. Whenever I hear talks about using our gifts, I wonder whether I have any. But recently I came across a useful tool on the internet that gives additional definitions to five key gifts, which enabled me to have a clearer understanding as to my own gifts.* The five gifts are also described as: light-giver (teacher); storyteller (evangelist) heart-revealer (prophet); soul-healer (pastor); dream-awakener (apostle). I took a survey and came up as a storyteller. I have never thought of myself as an evangelist but what I can do, and what I do naturally anyway, is to tell stories about what God is doing in my life in my poems and my blog and this connects with people.

We sow seeds in our own lives too. Sometimes there is a dream or a long-term project that we have sown into for a long time without any perceivable return. I have an unpublished novel on my laptop that I started ten years ago. I still have faith that it might get somewhere someday, but meanwhile I'm still writing. Let's not doubt that God is working through us. All He asks of us is to walk with Him and to stay connected – then we will be spreading kingdom seeds without even trying.

For prayer and reflection

Lord, thank You for all the seeds that I have sown in my life without even realising it. Use me to spread even more. Amen.

*fivefoldministrytest.com

Seeing: hide and **seek**

Luke 12:29–34

'seek his kingdom, and these things will be given to you as well.' (v31)

Seeking is active. Think of the childhood game hide and seek, and the intention that goes with seeking – moving cushions, crawling under beds, peering into the backs of wardrobes. Imagine if we sought the things of God with this much intention. If we seek *first* His kingdom, before everything else, then our focus is on Him first and foremost. Our focus is not on our career, financial rewards or status. That's not to say these things won't be added to us, but it is not what comes first. Seek the kingdom *first*, and everything else is in God's hands and timing. Paul says, 'You were running a good race. Who cut in on you…?' (Gal. 5:7) and sometimes this can be true for us. Has duty, obligation, insecurity or something else cut in on our race? A moving interview with Nadim Ednan-Laperouse, whose daughter died of an allergic reaction to a sandwich in the UK, said that he had everything in life (he was a wealthy business owner with an MBE), but after the tragedy, which led to a radical encounter with God, he said of his previous life and all that he had attained: 'I look back at all that now and none of it matters, its completely irrelevant.'* Through the most tragic of circumstances, he had found what was the most important. Jesus says, 'life does not consist in an abundance of possessions' (Luke 12:15). Status and wealth are not the measures of a life well-lived, not by God's standards. He sees the secret acts of kindness, the seeds sown in tears, the years of faithful prayers. God looks at the heart.

For prayer and reflection

Father, have I stopped seeking Your kingdom before everything else? Show me what I have put before You and lead me back to Your ways. Amen.

* The whole interview can be heard at bbc.co.uk/sounds/play/m000cmsf

Hear: make space

....

Psalm 139

'when I awake, I am still with you' (v18)

How do you hear the voice of God in your life? What helps you draw near to Him? Do you make room to do those things? In normal times, if we haven't seen a certain friend for a while, we would invite them around for a cup of tea or meet for a meal. We would spend time together, sharing the big and the small things of our lives. But how often do we make space to be with God? Our lives will be what we make of them, and we make room for what is important. So, let's make room for God by lighting a candle, going for a walk under the trees, listening to the birds, standing on a beach and listening to the power of the waves. Let's talk to God by carving out a space where we can voice doubts and questions, joys and fears. My mum has a 'God chair' where she sits each day and asks if He has anything to say. Sometimes she hears something, sometimes not, but she still makes space each day.

This weekend spend some time with God, and take comfort in the words of this wonderful psalm that reminds us that there is nothing outside of Him, no distance too far to cross, no one too far gone for His love.

....

Optional further reading:

Margaret Silf, *Landmarks: An Ignatian Journey* (London: Darton, Longman and Todd Ltd, 1998)

Simply Church

– New Edition

By Sim Dendy

With new chapter on the Church in crisis, 'Weathering the Storm', written during Covid-19.

When crisis strikes – such as the Covid-19 pandemic – we have no choice but to stop and assess where we are. Our world needs the Church, like never before, to be full of hope. But the Church is not always what it could be. Perhaps we need a declutter. A clear-out. A detox.

This book is for all people who are passionate about the Church of Jesus Christ and seeing it continue to grow and serve.

We all collect excess stuff – books, clothes, cars, gadgets… thoughts, habits, scars, traditions… Sometimes, it's good to strip things back a bit. It's healthy to occasionally explore our past and consider a fresh purpose for the future.

To realign ourselves with the plan that our creator God has already set out for us.

To recalibrate.

To return to the start again.

To go back a couple of millennia to discover what the original Church looked like, so we can remember and reset.

Simply… Church.

To find out more and to purchase, visit **waverleyabbeyresources.org/sc**

Hear: be ever **hearing**

Mark 4:21–25

'If anyone has ears to hear, let them hear.' (v23)

When Jesus taught, there were many people who said that they didn't understand. It is good to ask questions because it is in the seeking that we receive revelation. The Passion Translation of verse 24 says, 'according to the depth of your longing to understand, much more will be added to you.' It strikes me that it isn't in striving that we receive revelation, but rather in taking time to be with God and turning to Him throughout our day. That 'depth of longing to understand' starts with the heart. Writing down any words that we receive from God is so important because, over time, it can change the course of our lives. Being led by God isn't one moment on one day, it is many every day over a lifetime. Frederick Buechner writes about the holy mystery of Jesus' teaching saying, 'God speaks to us in such a way, presumably, not because he chooses to be obscure but because, unlike a dictionary word whose meaning is fixed, the meaning of an incarnate word is the meaning it has for the one it is spoken to, the meaning that becomes clear and effective in our lives only when we ferret it out for ourselves.'* We learn when we immerse ourselves in Scripture, when we wrestle with it. And when the Word comes alive and we hear the voice of our shepherd, we write it down, we let the seed of it go deep into our hearts – we perhaps let it change the course of our life. We walk that new path because He is our good shepherd and we know His voice. He walks ahead, and we follow because we trust Him (John 10:3).

For prayer and reflection

Father, thank You for Your grace. Thank You that You will give us revelation after revelation when we come to You with ears to hear. Amen.

*Frederick Buechner, *Listening to Your Life* (New York: HarperCollins, 1992) p4

Hear: be like **children**

'Let the little children come to me… the kingdom of God belongs to such as these.' (v16)

L ittle children are innocent and playful; they live in the moment, they laugh often, they ask questions, they are teachable. Ray Simpson says that children 'sacramentalise the minutiae of the everyday with a flower here, a drawing there, a song for every occasion.' They haven't yet separated the sacred and the everyday. Speaking to His Father, Jesus says, 'you have hidden these things from the wise and learned, and revealed them to little children' (Matt. 11:25). The kingdom of heaven is not quickly understood like a set of rules, but rather grappling with riddles from the master storyteller and having a heart to learn. The kingdom of heaven is the upending of everything that society places value on. When society says money comes first, Jesus says, 'No, the heart is the most important.' When our culture yells at us to be faster, do more and be more productive, the gospels tell us to rest. Jesus encourages us to become like children: teachable and humble. He says, 'whoever welcomes one such child in my name welcomes me' (Matt. 18:5). Perhaps Jesus is saying pour out your love, even on those who will not necessarily bring you gain. Value everyone you meet, because the fingerprint of God is on them all. Jesus' disciples thought He was wasting His time on the children, but Jesus said let them come.

How do we see the holy in everything we do? We pay attention. We honour the sacred; we see the fingerprint of God in everything; we understand perhaps that even our heavenly Father is childlike in His playfulness. 'It may be that God… has the eternal appetite of infancy; for we have sinned and grown old; and our Father is younger than we.''

'Ray Simpson, *Exploring Celtic Spirituality* (Stowmarket, UK: Kevin Mayhew, 2008) p103

''Phillip Yancey *Soul Survivor* (London: Hodder and Stoughton, 1997) p64

For prayer and reflection

Lord, help me to be childlike, to be teachable, to live in wonder. Amen.

A **holy** deafness

Mark 5:35–43

'But Jesus refused
to listen to what
they were told'
(v36, TPT)

Jairus has just been told that his daughter had died,
but Jesus has a holy deafness to the news. He
knows that she will be healed. Sometimes we need
to have a holy deafness to things we hear. If we have a
seed from God – a promise for the salvation of a friend,
a business idea, or a long-harboured hope for healing –
then we need to hold on to it. Peter got out of the boat
and walked towards Jesus but when Peter started to
look around him at the impossibility of his situation, he
began to sink (Matt. 14:28–31). Sometimes the most
unbelievable things happen in our lives, and then,
somehow, we forget that they are a miracle because
they have become commonplace.

Our eldest daughter, Ivy, was diagnosed with Type
1 diabetes at the age of two. I remember the doctor
saying, 'Her pancreas is dying', but something in me
rejected that. A few years later, there was a longing in
me for another child. I could see her in my dreams: a
little girl, called Annie. I felt like she was waiting in the
wings, wondering if there was room for her to come and
join in. But we were scared that we wouldn't be able to
cope, and I was worried about judgment from others.
Then I had a miscarriage, and I thought, *Lord, have I
heard You wrong?* I became pregnant again, and we
prayed our way through nine months. Finally, Annie
was here. Sometimes the thing you have longed for
can become normal, boring, stressful even. Annie is
the answer to many prayers. Her existence enables
us to continue praying and holding on for a cure or a
new therapy for Ivy that would regenerate her insulin
producing cells.

**For prayer
and reflection**

**Lord, is there
anything You are
asking me to have
a holy deafness
about? Help me to
hold onto the
words You have
spoken. Amen.**

Hear: **cling** to the Word

Luke 8:5–15

'those lovers of truth… hear it deep within their hearts' (v15, TPT)

Within the seed lies life. There is a choice here. *Do I want to go deeper with God? Do I want to take what He says to me seriously?* In this parable, sometimes the ground was hard and not ready to receive the Word of God; sometimes the seed started to sprout and then got choked by weeds; another time, it didn't have roots deep enough to reach the life-giving water in the ground. But the 'lovers of truth' have responded by 'clinging to the word'. We are responsible for stewarding the seeds that have been dropped into our spirits.

Sitting here writing these notes as I approach my forties, I realise that actually I have trusted God's calling for me to pursue my writing above any other career. I have learned that listening is not about hearing one time the one thing that God is calling you to do (although sometimes we wish it could be that straightforward), rather listening is something that you do over and over. I am finally reaching a place in my life where I can see the fruit of stewarding God's Word in my life. There were times when I thought I should get a 'proper' job, not be a freelance writer. There have been times when we have felt utterly lost with no idea what our future would look like. There have been times when we have switched off for a season and become disappointed because what the world has to offer isn't enough for us. We have tasted heaven and, after that, nothing else is enough. We sometimes have to make sacrifices to hold on to God's Word but knowing Him as a friend who walks alongside us is the true and deep joy that surpasses all else.

For prayer and reflection

Lord, thank You that Your seed of truth grew in me. Thank You that it is flourishing in me even if it doesn't feel like it all the time. Amen.

Hear: live **vital** lives

John 15:1–8

'If you remain in me and I in you, you will bear much fruit; apart from me you can do nothing.' (v5)

I met up with a missionary connected with our church a few years ago to talk about writing and faith. I remember the fire in her eyes when she talked about what she was living for. I remember her saying we need to be living 'vital lives'. And that is the thing, isn't it? We want to know that our lives are vital, meaningful, necessary. I love this vision of Jesus being the vine, our very life source. We can do nothing unless we are filled with His life. Sometimes, it is wiser to take on less and do it well, rather than try to juggle too much and do it badly. Every year in January, I look back through my journals and make a list of all the things I wanted to achieve the previous year, and then I tick off the ones that I managed to do. It is encouraging when I can tick things off, but it also gives me a list for the next year if there were things that didn't get done.

Sometimes it's helpful for us to reflect on how we spend our time. Are the areas we invested our time fulfilling? Do they bear fruit in our lives? Is God asking us to lay any of these things down to concentrate on something else? Some things are right for a season and then they start to feel ill-fitting, that's just the way life is. Verse 2 says, 'He cuts off every branch in me that bears no fruit'. This might sound harsh until coupled with the second half, and then we understand that pruning is love. By taking away the branches that are draining us, the energy can be directed to the branches that are bearing fruit. God is a loving gardener and in His hands we are safe.

For prayer and reflection

Ask Jesus now if there is any branch He needs to prune away in you. Remember that you are safe in His hands. Amen.

Feel: let go

Psalm 4

'In peace I will lie down and sleep, for you alone, LORD, make me dwell in safety.' (v8)

Sometimes, I can't sleep at night. I lie there with the worries of the day running through my mind. Carrying unresolved problems or worries can sometimes lead to stress, insomnia and other chronic conditions. It is important to let issues come to the surface and work through them – they won't go away if they are buried. When I am struggling with something, I journal, I go for walks, I talk with friends, I pray. I have also just started doing Pilates, which really helps me to let go of any tension in my body. Whatever your method, work to establish healthy ways of letting go of worry. Somerset Maugham says of the writer, 'Whenever he has anything on his mind… he has only to put it down in black and white… to forget all about it. He is the only free man.'*

Take a moment today to reflect on how you are feeling. Be aware of any heartache or worry. Be aware of anyone you need to forgive. Release forgiveness to them.

Optional further reading:

Henri J.M. Nouwen, *The inner voice of love* (London: Darton, Longman and Todd, 1997)

'Somerset Maugham, *Cakes and Ale* (London: William Heinemann, 1930)

Feel: **peace** for weariness

**Matthew
11:25–30**

'Come to me, all
you who are weary
and burdened, and
I will give you rest.'
(v28)

F ollowing on from the weekend's theme of letting
go of worry, we turn to this invitation from
Jesus to exchange our burdens for His peace.
Sometimes painful situations go on for a long time. We
can keep bringing them back to our loving Lord every
day if we need to.

As I was re-reading the Gospels, I noticed the number
of times that Jesus says, 'Do not be afraid' (Matt. 28:10;
Luke 12:32; John 14:27) or as it is translated in the
Passion Translation, 'Don't yield to fear' (John 14:27).
It is a temptation, but fear is something that we don't
have to bear. As I'm writing, the world is living through
the coronavirus pandemic and many have lost loved
ones. Right now, fear is very real. Hospitals have been
stretched to capacity, jobs have been lost, education
disrupted and retail companies have collapsed. It is a
time where fear is real and a time where we have had to
take real precautions.

When Jesus invites us to come to Him, to give Him
our heaviness, our depression, our anxiety, we get to
walk away with peace. Matthew 6:26 says, 'Look at the
birds'; see how they live – unfettered, carefree in the
care of God.

Anxious thoughts may come, but we have a choice
in how we respond to them. Jesus says in John 14:27,
'I do not give to you as the world gives.' His peace is
otherworldly and can transform our lives. The peace
that He gives isn't only for when life is perfect; it is for
every day, for the midst of struggle, for the midst of
whatever you are facing right now. It is the antidote
to fear. As light is to dark, peace is to fear. This is the
sacred everyday.

**For prayer
and reflection**

**Lord, I come to You
today and bring
You my pain, fears
and unease. By
Your grace, please
exchange them for
Your peace. Amen.**

Feel: put down **roots**

Mark 4:30–32

'It is like a mustard seed, which is the smallest of all seeds on earth.' (v31)

Fear may shake us, but if we have allowed the seed of the kingdom to grow in us, then, like a tree, we shall be rooted in the storms. Margaret Silf writes, 'It is a wise and blessed soul that doesn't waste itself running after the whims of the moment and joining in the gossip of the marketplace. Such a soul is like a tree planted beside living water, putting down deep roots to where its true nourishment is found.'*

When a tree goes through a season of adversity, it doesn't grow much, but in the long run, this actually makes the tree stronger as its rings grow closer together. Difficult seasons are often learning grounds. Think back to a hard time in your life, what did it produce in you? Resilience, rest, a return to that deep root, your life source? In the same way, let the kingdom grow in us. Let our roots go down into the soil. Let the smallest seed become a tree in our lives – bigger than life itself – in the seeds of kindness that we sow around us and the stories we tell of our life with Jesus. Frederick Buechner writes about the possibilities of letting the seed of the kingdom grow in us, far beyond anything we could have imagined: 'And deep in my heart I do believe we shall overcome some day, as he will, by God's grace, by helping the seed of the kingdom grow in ourselves and in each other until finally in all of us it becomes a tree where the birds of the air can come and make their nests in our branches. That is all that matters really.'**

For prayer and reflection

Lord, help me to put down my roots deep into the stream. Help me to know Your truth deep within me. Help me return to You, the source of my life when times are hard. Amen.

*Margaret Silf, *Landscapes of Prayer* (Oxford: Lion Hudson, 2011) p38

**Frederick Buechner, *Listening to Your Life* (New York: HarperCollins, 1992) p229

Touch: acts of **love**

Luke 10:30–37

'But a Samaritan…
came where the
man was;
and when he saw
him, he took pity
on him.' (v33)

How can we show our love practically? How can we bring the sacred into the way that we interact with others? In today's parable, the Samaritan went against cultural norms to help this man. Kindness to strangers is love and can bring blessing.

Guidelines during lockdown prevent us from us from going into the homes of those we love or touching anyone that we don't live with. A hug from a friend now seems a very precious thing that previously we took for granted. The way we are called to live is to honour life, to show love however and whenever we can, to forgive, to show mercy, to stand up against injustice. During the pandemic, many people all over the world pulled together, delivering food and medicines to the medically vulnerable, as a beautiful example of love.

Let's ask ourselves today if there's anything we can do to show our love practically. Let's be open to the Holy Spirit's leading. Living in the sacred everyday isn't about doing everything and becoming overwhelmed, neither is it about being perfect (that's impossible!), it's about turning to God. If you have a prompting in your heart to do something for someone, then aim to do it today (if possible). That act of kindness may be really timely for that person. The parable of the Good Samaritan also illustrates how important it is to be aware of the needs of others. The love of God *notices* where help is needed and acts upon it. It doesn't stay silent in the face of injustice. What is in your hands today? What are you equipped to be able to do? Ask God how He can use it for His glory.

**For prayer
and reflection**

Lord, help me to
open my eyes and
see how I can help
those around me.
Amen.

JUL/AUG 2021

JULY
GENTLENESS*
HANNAH HEATHER

AUGUST
ABRAHAM AND SARAH*
NICKI COPELAND

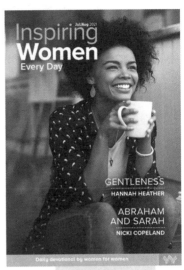

Available in a variety of formats.

In **July**, Hannah Heather looks at what it really means to be gentle and how powerful Spirit-filled gentleness can be.

In **August**, Nicki Copeland looks at the story of Abraham and Sarah and reflects on the twists and turns of life.

*Provisional titles

Obtain your copy from waverleyabbeyresources.org or from Christian bookshops.

Touch: be ever **knocking**

Luke 18:1–8

'And will not God bring about justice for his chosen ones, who cry out to him day and night?' (v7)

absolutely love this parable. You can just picture the widow knocking on the door, and the judge shouting, 'FINE!', and giving her what she wants, just so he would have a bit of peace and quiet. How much more does our heavenly Father long to answer the prayers of His children? There is a footnote in the Passion Translation saying that the Greek text uses an unusual verb which translates as 'ever tapping'. Sometimes in our desperation we dare to do the unheard of, the inappropriate, just like this widow. Let's be 'ever knocking' in our relationship with Jesus; let's keep telling Him about our dreams and heart cries. Let's keep on praying. We might think it's rude to keep asking (and God doesn't forget our prayers), but Jesus is literally inviting us here to be ever tapping.

There is a parallel story in Luke 11:5–10 where a man goes to his neighbour's house asking for food to give to some unexpected visitors. Jesus says, 'But listen— because of your shameless impudence, even though it's the middle of the night, your friend will get up out of his bed and give you all that you need. So it is with your prayers' (vv8–9). Jesus is encouraging us to have this 'shameless impudence'. So, I knock for the healing of my daughter. I knock for a novel to be published. I knock for my friends to come to know God. I knock for my friends who are facing difficult situations. With our prayers, we are pulling the kingdom of heaven down into our midst, carrying on with shameless impudence – just like we have been invited to.

For prayer and reflection

Lord, give us new prayers to pray when we are tired of praying, give us strength to keep the light of hope alive in our hearts. Amen.

Touch: **giving** all we have

Luke 21:1–4

'she sacrificed out of her poverty and gave to God all that she had to live on.' (v4)

I can just imagine the widow in this story, shuffling in, embarrassed by how little she had to give, but Jesus' eyes are on her. His eyes are on us too. Jesus sees our offerings – of money, time and service – and no matter how small they are by the world's standards, He sees our sacrifice. Each time we put our offering on the altar and say, 'God, this is all for You,' He sees it.

Before I had children, I used to lead worship with my husband. After I had my son, I tried to rejoin the worship team. But my son wouldn't go to a friend so that I could sing, he just wanted me. He wouldn't stay still with the other children, he was always running for the exits. I tried everything but in the end I had to give up leading worship for a season as it just wasn't working. I remember walking out of the church in tears one week because this decision seemed to reinforce a slow erosion of my character due to motherhood. However, I felt God say to me, 'I see you. I can see your sacrifice,' and it was a huge comfort.

God sees your sacrifice today. He doesn't see as the world sees. He sees you. Jesus talks a lot about money in the Gospels, and I think it is one of the areas where we can be a light in the world. Jesus specifically asks us to be generous, to pay our tithe and to bless others with gifts. 'It is important that you use the wealth of this world to demonstrate your friendship with God by winning friends and blessing others' (Luke 16:9, TPT). Money can easily become an idol, whether we have too much or too little of it, but when offered to God, money can be sanctified and used for His glory.

For prayer and reflection

Thank You, Father, that You see our offerings, that You see our best intentions. Thank You that nothing is wasted when it is done in service to You. Amen.

Fragrance

....

Matthew 26:6–13

'Why are you bothering this woman? She has done a beautiful thing to me.' (v10)

Whenever we do something for Jesus, we are like this woman, anointing Him with our lives. The onlookers said, 'Why this waste?' as she poured the equivalent of a year's salary on Jesus' feet. People may feel this about our lives too. We may offend them with the choices we have made. Our whole lives are for God's glory. Whether washing up or worshipping, 'we are to God the pleasing aroma of Christ' (2 Cor. 2:15). This 'aroma of Christ' might be in the things that we say, the way we spend our money or the way we have shaped our lives to glorify God. People may notice, and either they will want to know more, or shake their heads with disbelief.

It is far more important that our lives smell beautiful to God than that they look impressive on the outside. As Brother Lawrence reminds us, 'Our sanctification does not depend upon some alteration in what we do, but in doing for God what we commonly do for ourselves.' We need do nothing new, but do all that we do for Him.

....

Optional further reading:

Brother Lawrence, *The Practice of the Presence of God* (London: Hodder and Stoughton, 1981)
Douglas Kaine McKelvey, *Every Moment Holy* (Nashville: Rabbit Room Press, 2019)

'Brother Lawrence, *The Practice of the Presence of God* (London: Hodder and Stoughton, 1981) p29

Taste: **salt**

Matthew 5:1–13

'You are the salt of the earth.' (v13)

For the last three readings of this month, we will be thinking about taste. Jesus says we are to be salt – the tang that stays in the mouth and brings a dish to life. If we are salty, we are memorable, we stand out, we purify. How can we do this? By asking ourselves, do we put kingdom values first, instead of wanting to be liked or wanting to blend in? As we saw in the parable of the Good Samaritan on 23 June, part of showing the kingdom of heaven to others is by noticing needs and being proactive when possible. We are called to actively speak up against oppression and injustice. This might have a bearing on where we shop, who we vote for, what we protest about and all sorts of other things. Do we support independent retailers or big shops because they are cheaper?

In lockdown, instead of buying stuff, many turned to the simpler pleasures of life: sowing seeds, gardening or walking. For so long we have been sold the lie through advertising that what we have isn't good enough and that we need to update: bigger house, newer car, more holidays. But the more we walk with God, staying in Him like the branch stays in the vine, the more peace we will have about our decisions. We can often be apologetic for speaking about our faith because we don't want to offend, but Jesus says we are to 'freely declare in public' that He is the son of man (Luke 12:8, TPT). So, let us be salt when we speak boldly and graciously to others. 'Let your conversation be always full of grace, seasoned with salt, so that you may know how to answer everyone' (Col. 4:6).

For prayer and reflection

Lord, give us boldness to speak about You. Help us remain true to You, true to our character, authentic through and through. Amen.

Taste: come and **drink**

John 7:37–39

'Jesus stood and said in a loud voice, "Let anyone who is thirsty come to me and drink."' (v37)

We are human beings, we get thirsty. We get tired, demotivated and discouraged. Jesus says, 'Come to me and drink.' He has everything we need for life, and when we drink, a fountain flows within us. This living water, which is awakened within us, is poured out in our lives: 'Whoever believes in me, as Scripture has said, rivers of living water will flow from within them' (v38). Those around us are given a taste of this fresh water but to find the source of it for themselves, they need to go to Jesus. When Jesus met a woman at a well. He said, 'the water I give... will become... a spring of water welling up to eternal life' (John 4:14). Jesus encourages us to draw life from Him, to grow in faith and be transformed. This is the joy of the gospel, our faith, no matter how small, has the capacity to grow, to develop, to expand and to overflow in we keep drinking His water of life. Yeast, mustard seeds, a cup of water – they all start out so small. But all God is looking for is for us to say yes to Him. That is our part of the deal. We say yes, we give Him room, and the rest is heaven unfolding in our lives on earth – with amazing mystery and the poetry. Jesus' words are the perfect antidote to the voice of the world that says you'll never have enough. He says, 'Come, the well will never run dry, I have everything that you'll ever need.' So, let us come to Jesus today and ask for a cup of that refreshing water. Let us drink deeply, like the tree by the stream, soaking our roots in the truth of His Word.

For prayer and reflection

Lord, thank You that You invite us, again and again, to drink from Your life-giving water. May it well up in us, causing Your love to overflow in us. Amen.

Walk **humbly**

Micah 6:6–8

'what does the
LORD require...?
To act justly... to
love mercy... to
walk humbly with
your God.' (v8)

Jesus came down to be one of us, to live as we do with pain and joy. He saw the beauty of a sunset and held a flower in His hand. He ruffled the hair of a child. He saw His friends die. Let us live in step with Him. Let us know Him as our friend. Let us see through this beautiful world, and the eternal and mysterious words of the Gospels, that He is fully in touch with us right now. We have not been left as orphans, but He has given us the Holy Spirit to keep in touch with heaven – a divine and unbroken link. The Gospels show us that God is with us every day, we just need to be attuned to His voice. Frederick Buechner says, 'Listen to your life. See it for the fathomless mystery that it is. In the boredom and the pain of it no less than in the excitement and gladness: touch, taste, smell your way to the holy and hidden heart of it because in the last analysis all moments are key moments, and life itself is grace.'* There is no separating the two intertwined roots of the sacred and the everyday, the tears and the joy, the tantrums and sunsets, the miracles and sleepless nights. How does God measure a life well-lived? A life poured out, like that perfume, 'wasted' in loving and serving the 'least of these brothers and sisters of mine' (Matt. 25:40). Loving without limit; turning the wisdom of the world on its head. As Teilhard de Chardin wrote, 'God is not remote from us. He is at the point of my pen, my pick, my paint brush, my needle – and my heart and my thought.'**

*Frederick Buechner, *Listening to Your Life* (New York: HarperCollins, 1992) p2

**Teilhard de Chardin, *Hymn of the Universe* (New York: Harper & Row, 1965) p84

Notes

Order form

Get Your FREE Daily Bible Reading Notes TODAY! (UK ONLY)

Your favourite Bible reading notes are now FREE. God has called us back to the original vision of CWR to provide these notes to everyone who needs them, regardless of their circumstance or ability to pay. It is our desire to see these daily Bible reading notes used more widely, to see Christians grow in their relationship with Jesus on a daily basis and to see Him reflected in their everyday living. Clearly there are costs to provide this ministry and we are trusting in God's provision.

Could you be part of this vision? Do you have the desire to see lives transformed through a relationship with Jesus? **A small donation from you of just £2 a month, by direct debit, will make such a difference** Giving hope to someone in desperate need whilst you too grow deeper in your own relationship with Jesus.

4 Easy Ways To Order

1. Visit our online store at **waverleyabbeyresources.org/store**
2. Send this form together with your payment to: **CWR, Waverley Abbey House, Waverley Lane, Farnham, Surrey GU9 8EP**
3. Phone in your credit card order: **01252 784700** (Mon–Fri, 9.30am – 4.30pm)
4. Visit a Christian bookshop

For a list of our National Distributors, who supply countries outside the UK, visit waverleyabbeyresources.org/distributors

Your Details (required for orders and donations)

Full Name:

CWR ID No. (if known):

Home Address:

Postcode:

Telephone No. (for queries):

Email:

Publications

TITLE	QTY	PRICE	TOTAL
	TOTAL PUBLICATIONS		

UK P&P: up to £24.99 = **£2.99**; £25.00 and over = **FREE**

Elsewhere P&P: up to £10 = **£4.95**; £10.01 – £50 = **£6.95**; £50.01 – £99.99 = **£10**; £100 and over = **£30**

Total Publications and P&P (please allow 14 days for delivery)   **A**

Payment Details

☐ I enclose a cheque made payable to CWR for the amount of: **£**

☐ Please charge my credit/debit card.

Cardholder's Name (in BLOCK CAPITALS)

Card No.

Expires End   Security Code

Continued overleaf >>

One off Special Gift to CWR ☐ Please send me an acknowledgement of my gift **B**

GRAND TOTAL (Total of A & B)

Gift Aid (your home address required, see overleaf)

giftaid it I am a UK taxpayer and want CWR to reclaim the tax on all my donations for the four years prior to this year **and on** all donations I make from the date of this Gift Aid declaration until further notice.*

Taxpayer's Full Name (in BLOCK CAPITALS) _____

Signature _____ **Date** _____

*I am a UK taxpayer and understand that if I pay less Income Tax and/or Capital Gains Tax than the amount of Gift Aid claimed on all my donations in that tax year it is my responsibility to pay any difference.

Your FREE Daily Bible Reading Notes Order

	Please Tick	FREE	£2 pcm	£5 pcm	£10 pcm	Other
Every Day with Jesus		☐	☐	☐	☐	☐ £ _____
Large Print *Every Day with Jesus*		☐	☐	☐	☐	☐ £ _____
Inspiring Women Every Day		☐	☐	☐	☐	☐ £ _____

All CWR Bible reading notes are also available in single issue **ebook** and **email subscription** format. Visit **waverleyabbeyresources.org** for further info.

CWR Instruction to your Bank or Building Society to pay by Direct Debit

DIRECT Debit

Please fill in the form and send to: CWR, Waverley Abbey House, Waverley Lane, Farnham, Surrey GU9 8EP

Name and full postal address of your Bank or Building Society

To: The Manager _____ Bank/Building Society

Address _____

_____ Postcode _____

Name(s) of Account Holder(s)

Branch Sort Code

Bank/Building Society Account Number

Originator's Identification Number

4	2	0	4	8	7

Reference

Instruction to your Bank or Building Society

Please pay CWR Direct Debits from the account detailed in this Instructi subject to the safeguards assured by the Direct Debit Guarantee. I understand that this Instruction may remain with CWR and, if so, details will be passed electronically to my Bank/Building Society.

Signature(s)

Date

Banks and Building Societies may not accept Direct Debit Instructions for some types of account

For a subscription outside of the UK please visit www.waverleyabbeyresources.org where you will find a list of our national distributors.

How would you like to hear from us? We would love to keep you up to date on all aspects of the CWR ministry, including; new publications, events & courses as well as how you can support us.

If you **DO** want to hear from us on email, please tick here [ ] If you **DO NOT** want us to contact you by post, please tick here [
You can update your preferences at any time by contacting our customer services team on 01252 784 700. You can view our privacy policy online at waverleyabbeyresources.org

Insight

Helping you and helping others

Mental health and emotional health is something we really care about at Waverley Abbey Resources. Our Insight range is designed for people who are facing struggles themselves or who are supporting others.

Online courses

Insight is now online! We have launched our online courses and will continue to add to these so that you can, at your own pace, spend time understanding these topics that affect so many of us.

Books

Our range of books cover many topics and include Christian wisdom, theory and real-life examples, so that you can steps forward.

Devotionals

Every Day Insights are devotionals that will help you to connect with God right where you are, whilst finding understanding and wisdom surrounding particular topics.

Visit **waverleyabbeyresources.org/insight** to find out more

Inspiring Women Every Day is written by women, for women, to help build faith and bring encouragement to your daily walk with God.

THE YES'S OF GOD

Rachel Wright looks at the Bible not as a list of no's, as some people see it, but a call to yes's, and explores:

- the times in the Bible when God said yes
- the women of faith in Scripture who said yes to God
- how relationship with Jesus is more about freedom than restriction.

THE SACRED EVERYDAY

Elisabeth Pike reflects upon how the ordinary, even mundane moments can be sacred and shows that:

- our everyday moments can be given to God in worship
- time is a previous gift that we can use for God and for good
- the life-giving presence of God is always available to us.

waverleyabbeyresources.org

f /WAinspiringwomen

ISBN 978-1-78951-323-3

9 781789 513233

ALSO AVAILABLE AS
EMAIL SUBSCRIPTION/EBOOK/KINDLE

WAVERLEY ABBEY
RESOURCES

Trading name of **CWR**